CW01212960

salmonpoetry

Diverse Voices from Ireland and the World

Also by Noel Monahan

Poetry

Opposite Walls (Salmon, 1991)
Snowfire (Salmon,l995)
Curse of the Birds (Salmon, 2000)
The Funeral Game (Salmon, 2004)
Curve of the Moon (Salmon, 2010)
Where The Wind Sleeps: New & Selected Poems (Salmon, 2014)
Celui qui Porte Un Veau / The Calf-Bearer
(Translated by Emmanuel Malherbet (France: L'Arbre, 2014)
Chalk Dust (Salmon, 2018)

Plays

Half A Vegetable. A dramatic presentation of Patrick Kavanagh's poetry and performed by Temenos Theatre, 1994.
Feathers of Time. Performed at Ramor Theatre by St. Clare's College.
Broken Cups. Directed by Aidan Matthews, for RTE Radio Drama, 2002.
Talking Within. Directed by Padraic McIntyre, at Ramor Theatre, 2003.
Where Borders Begin. Commissioned by Cavan County Council, 2004.
To Walk On The Wind. Performed at Ramor Theatre, by St. Clare's College.
The Children of Lir. Directed by Padraic McIntyre, for Livin Dred Theatre, 2007.
Lovely Husbands. Commissioned by the Henry James Festival Committee, 2010.
Chalk Dust. Stage Adaption by Noel Monahan and Directed by Padraic McIntyre, 2019.

As Editor

Badal. Knocknarea Writers Anthology
Garden of Golden Apples. An anthology of students of St. Daigh's School, Inniskeen, Co. Monaghan.
Writing Across Borders. A collection of original poetry from Writers' Groups living in Ireland's Border Region, 2012.
Frank Miller Stole My Girl. An Anthology of Poetry by LITLAB, 2017.
Chasing Shadows, A Miscellany of Poetry. Longford County Library, 2022.

As Co-Editor

Windows Publications. Authors &Artists Series Nos.1- 11. Co-Edited with Heather Brett.

Journey Upstream

Poems by

NOEL MONAHAN

salmonpoetry

Published in 2024 by
Salmon Poetry
Cliffs of Moher, County Clare, Ireland
Website: www.salmonpoetry.com
Email: info@salmonpoetry.com

ISBN 978-1-915022-59-2

Cover & Title Page Image: *River Painting 2* by *Padraig Lynch*
Cover Design & Typesetting: Siobhán Hutson

Printed in Ireland by Sprint Print

Salmon Poetry gratefully acknowledges the support of
The Arts Council / An Chomhairle Ealaíon

the arts council an chomhairle ealaíon
funding literature
artscouncil.ie

for Oisín, Fiadh and Lyla

Contents

Sol and Luna

for Anne

I
Stood on
The sun, she
Stood on the moon
And time gripped the two of us together
We live our lives dissolving from then on
Not knowing our
Beginning
And the
End

Journey Upstream

Erne

I

I am the music of water flowing
From the hills. I have many forms and guises,
I fling open the doors to the lakes:
Gowna, Uachtair and my namesake Erne.
I love to dance, I vary my rhythms of flow.
I am pagan and Christian
I am earth and I am sky
When the sun shines
                    I clothe myself in clouds.
My name is Erne, the primordial one,
I was born geo ages ago,
Old enough to know all that I am.
My love song is: *Buachaill Ón Éirne*,
My breath's the wind, my mind
Is never far from the moon.

Erne

II

I flow deeper than you can imagine.
Tired of everyday tasks:
Coming from here and going there ...
I love the night sky of moon and stars,
Drop down
                    To my river bed.
I'll disrobe for you. Honeymoon with me
Under my limestone blankets,
Wallow in an underworld of dream wisdom,
Watch my shadows deepen, my thighs
Spill across a dreamland of drowned drumlins.
Tell your secrets to the moon and me.
I promise I'll kiss you with my parted lips,
Soothe and heal your wounds under the moon.

Journey Upstream

for Jessie Lendennie, Founder of Salmon Poetry

Never one for fad, fame and fashion,
You held your finger on the pulse of time,
Sniffed out the magic of verse
At home in your Zach and Zookie world
Of *Singing Dogs*
                    You created a new myth:
Reconnected us with the Salmon
Brought us back in time to
Mountain berries dropping into a well
Where Finn the boy burnt his thumb
Sucked it better and solved the mystery
Of the journey of souls, journey of salmon,
Journey of going home with an inimitable
Jessie Lendennie chuckle.

Aphrodite in the Snow

I awaken to the surprise of seeing you
Stretched naked outside my window,
Your ivy hair full of snowflakes,
Earrings of frozen ice, blizzard of pearl powder
For your face. Fresh snow begins to blow
Across your navel, curves about your pubic bones,
Lodges between your thighs.
                                                  I know you drifted here.
The wind shaped your limbs, your snow white girdle
And now the wind of forty voices sings:
Spem In Alium in the snow,
Choral whispers of hope in the singing bowl of winter.
A car passes with head-lights on, someone is scraping a driveway
And I'm not sure whether I'm looking at the evening or morning star.

Nuns’ Graveyard

Killashee, Co. Kildare

How peaceful it is, grey enclosed walls,
Dark metal crosses mark the dead,
Barely remembered, except for religious names:
Sister Martha, Sister Angela ...
I try to picture them now, porcelain nuns’ faces
Chanting across a chalk-line of time,
All their teaching head-aches over
All daughters of Christ once,
Their souls now fly with the swallows
And life moves on.
We have fallen crazily in love with ourselves
Our phones our cameras, we live in the iPad, iPhone
Moment, taking photos of the nuns’ graves today
Barely remembering them tomorrow.

Advice to a Young Poet

i.m. Tom MacIntyre

Break the lock on the field gate,
Avoid the muck-worms at the gap,
Abandon old visions you have of yourself:
Self pity in the face of a terrible God,
The tribe of ghosts constantly shouting.
Get to meet God's strange people living there:
The silenced priest, the lost child...
                    Stay in the field with its mysteries
Sift through the grass with the brown hare
Listen to the hills clapping hands,
Crab apples dropping into the ditch.
If you remain long enough
You'll feel the warmth of a candle burning inside you,
The blur of its flame constantly changing.

For Oisín

Born 18th April, 2018

Oisín, little deer, child from the land of youth,
Golden-haired, blue-eyed, lungs of laughter,
Forever watching our lip movements,
Jigsaw of sounds to be pieced into words,
Your hands constantly shifting from soft toys
To pillows, the odd whimper for milk on demand.
You leave your mark with us
                                        Hand and foot in the sand
Forever framed on the mantelpiece.
Oisín, Oisín, we call your name across
Seas of sleep on your bedroom wall
To shifts of shadows, curtain of dreamlands
And the rattle and rhythm of your hearty laugh
In Tír na nÓg.

Smile on an Infant's Face

for Fiadh, born 28th February 2020

My name is Fiadh: *Wild Deer*
I am light-footed, the bones in my feet
Are graceful and growing,
Soon I will dance with the wind.
My eyes are sometimes misted by tears
But today they carry the sun.
My dreams are not revealed yet,
Somehow I know
                    I have the gaze of a beautiful girl.
My brother Oisín is a little deer
He waters the flowers with his watering-can
My Dad grew a beard for Covid-19,
My Mom loves the smile on my infant face,
I feed at dawn, fade by noon
Into a soul sleep in her arms.

Robin

response to a painting by Padraig Lynch

Robin, we meet again at Christmas time.
New Year hasn't yet arrived, last year just about over.
Timeless warrior, breast plate of orange, wild gae bolga eye,
You pierce me with that look of yours, inviting me
Across a rushy meadow of snow light to a distant ford
Of half forgotten history,
Where Cuchulain and Ferdia fought.
No one bothers you out here, cut off from parish news,
Your kingdom, a ceiling of blue snow clouds,
Over a grey chapel lost in the woodlands of snow.
You have that look of concern, perched down stage left,
You almost talk to me, coax me to grab a spade,
Clear the snow, dig clod and clay and let you forage
For your Christmas breakfast.

The Home Economics Room

in memory of Máire Clarke

We have our memories to colour our recall of you
Toing and froing in the Home Economics Room,
Aroma of cinnamon, coriander, cloves ...
A space of refinement and elegance:
Tureen of vegetable soup, salad bowls
And the engaged faces of the students
Looking up at you.
                                        Everything about the room
Speaks of your personality. A wonder room of your giving:
Basket of football and camogie jerseys beside the washing machine,
Student projects on healthy eating, pinned on the wall,
All the costumes for the TY Drama characters: *The Henwoman*,
The Brosnaman and *The Three Hail Marys*, all neatly folded
By your loving hands. Your inspiration Máire, lives on in St. Clare's
Like a poem that freely writes itself.

Grunewald's Painting on the Crucified Christ

Confession was a Catholic cure for sin
And we recalled Grunewald's haunted painting
Of the death of Christ: Mouth agape,
Crown of thorns, smear and spots on his skin,
Nailed contorted hands and feet,
A lamb with a sword-cross through its heart
Blood dripping into the Holy Grail.
What *word became flesh, dwelt amongst us?*
Driving us into dark confession boxes
Year after year after year...
Our heads in our hands, our accusatory demons
Shouting out loud: *When I was hungry, when I was thirsty...*
Now the noise of hammered nails is silent.
We no longer confess. We bear our guilt, carry it everywhere.

Light of Our Lives

for Lyla, born 12th March 2020

I arrived on a Covid clouded day,
But I'm becoming more myself by the hour.
I can breathe and I can eat, I have feelings in my feet.
Every now and then I raise a howl,
Mumble, grimace, routine release of wind...
I'm outwardly looking
                                        Beyond the minutes and hours
Beyond the colours of flowers on the patio.
I love all this pampering from my Mom and Dad,
My brothers and sister and I know my blue eyes
Make my grandparents smile. But for the moment
I'm looking at gentle sleep flowing down
From the hills and trees, sleep beyond
The lull of birdsong in the garden
Lyla asleep.

When You Are Alone in a House

You may hear voices, crashing noises of
Furniture being moved, someone swearing.
The language gets more and more obscene,
But remember, there's nobody up there in the attic,
Nobody's playing the piano down in the sitting room.
The voices and the noises outside you
Are really within you
                              Bottled up.
Something you fell prey to in the long ago.
Black thorn, white thorn, spine of porcupine
Prickling and niggling away at you in the mixing bowl,
Two sides of yourself at odds with each other
And you continue to live out your life
In the damp cold dark rooms of your home,
In the silence and noises of living on your own.

Temples of Time

Every Drumlin reminds me
Of Golgotha, a place of skulls,
Bony heads of hills, empty eye sockets,
Cocked ears listening to the wind and rain,
Rounded temples of time, once sacred to ice,
Grim virgins that defied our spades and shovels
For centuries.
                    But their time is spun out.
I see man's shadow climb down from the cross,
Lights out in heaven, no heat in hell.
These hills no longer make us happy,
No children, only ageing men and women
Long dark winter nights, silent voices
Alone by the fireside, the TV blaring .

Pull Down the House

Break down the doors and windows
Let the jackdaws fly out from the chimneys,
The mice leave their nests
Under the floorboards. Tear the wallpaper
In the bedrooms, pluck the weeds from the gutters,
Knock all the walls, send up clouds of lime and sand,
Cut down the trees, uproot the lawn
Leave not a forget-me-not
                                        Behind.
Heads brooding over a winter fire,
Tongues talking, stories walking.
And before you leave, throw a sop to the memory
Of Darky the dog. Let the winds atone
                              The rain wash the stone.

Mullinalaghta

for Simon Cadam

Place names to die for:
Hill of standing stones, Larkfield,
Pathway through the oaklands,
Grey ridge among the bushes, red hillock,
Lake of the calf, a horse meadow to run wild in.
Dinnseanchas of stones on the move,
From Inchmore to the Big House, to the chapel walls ...
A Mighty people all
                    At home with the lie of the land
Proud to don the maroon and white colours.
Our forwards are fast as hares
Our defence always firm footed
We have played against the greats
And beat the best.
Mullinalaghta, a homeland to live for.

Harvest Of Healing

A time of clay and water
When Brigid was loved and feared
And we knelt at the Clootie Well,
Tied ribbons and rags to a lone bush
And prayed Brigid would spare us.

Drills were lines on a green page
Poets gathered healing words from the fields,
Green chapels lit up with cowslips,
Candle light of fairy flax in the evenings,
Night-time, harebells rang out
To the nipplewort of Brigid's leaves unfolding.
A gust of wind came from nowhere and blew
A cloud of thistledown
                                        Into the next parish.

Knockbride

Highland of the gods and Brigid
Where Cornaveagh, Corleck and Skeagh
Hover like ghosts about bush and heather.
Shh... Listen for the songs and psalm-singers,
The moon-white whispers
                    Over Dubthach's ridge of death
A world out of darkness, apart from anywhere
Where the old and new faiths meet.

Beehive querns, water-stoop
Open book to sky, sun, moon and stars
Where the white cow grazes with her calves,
Hum of spinning wheels and looms
On Raven's Hill, highland
Of mysterious stones and Brigid.

A Beautiful Distraction

What inspired thought entered your head?
Drove you to look beyond yourself.
Was there some disaster, a disease spreading,
Famine in the long ago?

Did the sun set fire to your head?
Did you dream in the shadow of the moon?
Or were you utterly lost in a fog
Astray on the Corleck Hill?

Today onlookers stare in wonderment
At your empowering head with three faces
It's that beautiful distraction
They tirelessly crave and love:

Something to think about,
Something to talk about.

Still-Life

Response to Pádraig Lynch's painting

Still Life breathes quietly tonight.
Nothing moves.
This is a moment to be shared at Christmas:
An age old longing burns in our hearts,
We fear the globe will cough and spread
Shadows over us.
                    Candle flame,
Older than prayer itself
Reminds us of syllables of love,
An inner world gives us time to reconnect
With all that we've forgotten.
Random items remind us of
Fleeting time. All the colour,
Light and darkness probe and play with silence.

Schoolgirls

for Geraldine on her birthday

We remember another time in Salthill
When everything seemed to happen with laughter,
School voices, school bells, all the *Aves* and *Paters*
Before classes, with the Dominican Nuns,
Cycling there each morning
Meeting at the bottom of Glenard Avenue .
                                        We talked about everything,
Teased about boys, recalled our first drink at the disco,
More talk: cups of tea late at night
Our heads bent low to get that final exam.
Dreams, night skies of stars above the roof tops,
Sunset over Galway Bay:
Five female figures looking out to sea,
Five cormorants drying their wings
                                        Before they fly away.

Longing for the Stars

A Poem

Can talk to a child's heart
        Can walk with pilgrims' feet on stones,
Can open doors and windows
        Can be a sudden blessing in the dark
A hymn to your heart.

        A poem can weave words into dreams
Can be slow to grasp and understand
        Can be a branch forever tapping
                At your bedroom window.

Longing For The Stars

That cosmic need
To view a night's sky
Is alive in us all.

We never give up on finding
The great father, the eternal mother
Or the hunt for that magical *OTHER*
And we continue to live their death,
Die their lives with the stars.

Chain of Events

We hungered for something to love.
Unaware, we carried the past with us.
Ghostly surveyors dragged
        Chains through daisy fields,
Dropped pins on our dreams,
Their ghostly faces white in limelight
        To combat winter darkness.

Heather beards growled at the wind.
The hare with the red eye on her forehead
        Raced past bullán stones, graveyard stones,
Past Mulláns, Móiníns, meadows ...
She alone knew Poetry was lost to the fields.

We the subdued ones continued to pay rent
Let them take our land and our language
And we waited like flatworms
                For our heads to grow back.

When I Slept in Winter Snow

When I slept in winter snow
                                        A wolf howled,
Bitter cold gods
                                        Came out to pray,
Ghosts threw snowballs
                                        At the stars,
Pilgrims dressed as bee-keepers
                                        Walked past midnight
To a hive of snowflakes.

        Snow sat
                Quietly white at night,
        Snow talked
                To my childhood,
        Snow was a light left on
                throughout the darkness.

The Theatre of Covid-19

A sudden silence,
An unexpected turn of events,
Everything stops,
The world shuts down.

Words fail to catch their breath.
The Covid Plague is now live theatre,
All one big drama played out:
On the streets, in care homes, hospitals...
No rehearsals. The plague is now protagonist,
Actors and audience are one in this human tragedy.

We no longer walk the streets. We lick our wounds at home,
Afraid to look at one another, we peep round the gable to see
If the postman is coming. Many of us go to bed early
Get up late.

LITANY OF WORDS SAID OVER AND OVER: Repeat after me:
Wash your hands: Sneeze into the triangle of your elbow
Stay inside: ***Don't come out***

Six O' Clock News:
The Drama and Plague Continue:
The streets are empty,
Lines of closed coffins file past in lorries,
More words pour out of the American President's Mouth ...
We can see our illness more clearly now.
Frenzied priests dance after Mass
And it goes viral on the internet.
Our grandchildren stay outside
Press their tiny hands
Against a window pane.

Carnival figures in masks
Make for eerie street theatre.
We undress our souls, sanitise our phones,
Nouns and verbs are slow to mix
A poem sleeps.

Now we hear the true sound of words,
Not words as things but words as sounds,
Now listen to the chaos of all creation,
Poetry caught in the song
Of a pigeon's beat of its wings,
Somewhere between heaven and earth.

Cootehill

Cootehill is theatrical and witty,
A love story that speaks its name.
Coote the groom and Hill the bride married,
Made history, gave the town its fame.
    Linen markets full of sleep
    Linen sheets and pillow slips
    Dreams full of fields of blue bloom
    Of flax fun and flurry:
    Pulling, retting, scutching, hackling ...
Oh! The warp and weft of it all
Where Moravians, Presbyterians, Quakers settled
Spun, wove and praised God.

    Now Shoppers with facemasks on
                    Crowd super markets, mini markets ...
    Beer barrels line Maxwells Lane, nightfall on Chapel Lane,
    Feet shuffle, keys jingle in the dark,
    A lost soul looks up at the moon. The door closes,
    Someone coughs on Market Street.

Erica's Fairy Forest is truly magical
Black Lake looks across at the White Lake,
Drumlona Lough is silver-grey,
Leaf language from tree to tree in Bellamont Park
Where the stately home still stands.

When the poet Dermot Healy
    Enticed Footsbarn Theatre to Cootehill
    The town fell under its spell : *A Midsummer Night's Dream*
    Talk of more marriage, Theseus and Hippolyta this time.

    Cootehill is a love story that never ends
    It began when Charles Coote wed Frances Hill
    And gave the town its name and fame.

Response to the Painting "Row"

by Michael O'Dea (1986)

All the pent-up energy is out on
The corridor, shamelessly shouting for
A fight to begin. All the eyes and noses
Sense only too well
There's no social distancing here.
                    Cream calm walls.
Shudder of blue, red and navy jumpers ...
Masquerading styles of mullet heads
Stand around waiting for something to happen.
Laughter, mockery, rousers rousing the crowd,
Litany of catchcries: *Hit him... Give him a Thump...a Dunt... a Box ...*
"Love Your Enemy", is a lesson easily forgotten here.
The two boys trapped in their own hell
Are centre stage,
                    One of them points his finger,
A peace-maker, a referee stands between them.
All the dancing devils surround them:
What the hell do we care? Devils today, saints tomorrow
Nearly all are out of their cages by now,
Except for the Honours Maths class
That continues to work through the bedlam
What's nearly invisible, nearly inaudible
Is that inward fear of repercussions:

Too many of us, they can't expel all?
What will the Principal or Deputy Principal say?
Boys among boys, all bored to death with each other,
Boys with limited learning skills?
They'll let us off as soon as we say:
                                        Sorry, Sorry, Sorry...

Heading West

for Niall, Cian and Ronan

On the road from Cavan to Galway,
We struck a deal and stuck to it:
We play our CDs first:
Pearl Jam, Nirvana and R.E.M.
And when we get as far as Mountbellew, Dad,
You can switch to your Whale Music
Is that fair?

Pearl Jam's Eddie Vedder, rang out:
Elderly Woman Behind The Counter
As we passed through Granard.
R.E.M. *When the day is long and the night...*
Took us as far as Longford
Then we got locked inside Kurt Cobain's
Heart Shaped Box
And Dad's music took over and we were swallowed up,
Lodged in the whales' bellies.
For the rest of the journey.

We were winged horses of the deep
Leaping, diving, groaning ...
In the low hum of whale hymns:

Whales have no words for their songs,
Dad explained: *Their songs are old and deep,*
Where God and man meet.

That may be so, but they were oceans away
From our Pearl Jam, Nirvana, R.E.M.
Drops of rain started to fall,
Spray from the sea at Salthill
And we were happy to arrive.

Nobody Home

We peeped through a window,
        The moon, my shadow and me.
Nobody home.
        Mugs and plates on a table,
Empty chairs,
        A blue Milk of Magnesia bottle
Alongside a statue of the Virgin Mary
        On a shelf.
The floor hadn't been swept for years.

Encounter with Abraxas

Hail to a weirdly wonderful
Rooster-headed one,
Human body, crocodile feet,

Complete with shield and whip in hands.
Chanticleer at the crack of dawn
One of the greats from the past

With relevance for today.
Heavenly one, rooster from hell,
Lover of light flowing into darkness...

Cock – A – Doodle – Doo.

Athena

Nothing less than
A splitting headache
To her father Zeus.
Wing-beats of an owl at night,
Our breath of life,
Watchful wisdom,
Bestower of olives to Athens,
Queen of the Parthenon,
Demure, untouched by man,
Patron of same-sex love.

Cave of Cats

for Sheila and Seán

Tonight all hell breaks loose at Rathcroghan,
Ireland's gate to Hell.
What lies trapped within, breaks out at Hallowe'en.
Morrigan drives her chariot through frosty fields,
        Drawn by a one-legged chestnut mare,
Triple-headed creatures walk abroad,
                Birds burn the grass with their beaks,
Wild pigs tear up the fields and refuse to be counted.

All unknown graves open:
        Horse bits, pig bones, bronze cauldrons come
From below to mystify our lives,
        All the lost children, all those who made
Themselves safely dead walk abroad tonight.

All that lies hidden in the wardrobe of our minds
All strange beliefs seep from the Cave of Cats:
Everything running in... and out... of everything else,
The man to be King has mounted a white mare,
A procession of hags trawls the darkness
Intoning:
        Medb is the land and the land is Medb...
    The mantra goes on forever.

Lupin in November

She stands beyond time,
Out there on the patio,
Swan neck of stately flowers
Washed by November rain,

Lir's loveliest daughter
Hearing her brothers sing
Octave of notes, string of words,
Floral pearls of purple and white

Ghostly standing at the window.
Giving light, music and words
To the breath of life's mystery
On this dark November day.

Portrait of a Librarian

for Mary Carleton Reynolds on the occasion of her retirement, 2022.

You made the library a home for us all.
School children found space there to open a book,
Draw a circle and paint the sun.
Always a devoted librarian,
A custodian of that space in town where new ideas
Find a place, come and go at will.
You made light of hard work: pages of reports,
Working modules, emails awaiting immediate answers ...
Not one for the " CIÚNAS" or the *"ssh!"*
You loved to talk about a book, an author, a library event ...
You blossomed at all library gatherings: Readings, Exhibitions ...
We loved your flamboyant flair
Colour after colour of flowing fabric
You lovingly opened the door to a world of books,
A world of wonder and the imagination
A world of starry nights and the long shadow life casts
And our wish for you: A world of happiness.

Linus

for Linus McDonnell, raconteur and storyteller

Linus poured pints of ichor, shots of benediction oil
And walked on hallowed ground behind his bar,
Moving from one story to another:

This country has been propped up
By fabrication for years!
Yes!   Oh yes!
In every yes there is a no.
We must restore our country
To its original state of corruption
Mother church and Mother Ireland,
All the tyrannies, democracies and aristocracies,
Has anything changed?
The R.I.C. eyes, the ears of the British Government,
Network of informers,
All gathering intelligence,
Did I hear an empty glass rattle?

Linus knew each one by name,
All the mothers' sons, all the fathers' daughters,
The wounded and the healed,
Silent men in civil wars with themselves
And he entertained them with a smile, a story,
A flip of a drying cloth, a parade march, a salute
To a night full of stars.

Unhappy Hour

When crows were white
And Gorgon's blood revived the dead,
Silenus, the pot-bellied one
Mounted an ass, headed for the city

To meet Midas,
(Urban chairman of the golden handshakes)
And there at the market square,
He defended
His anti-natal thoughts:
The best thing for man
Is not to be born
And if alive
To die as soon as possible.

Christmas is an Endless Childhood

Tucked away under a pillow,
        Snow fills our dreams, place names call us home:
Ardee, Cavan, Granard ...
        A robin red-breast casts spells on Ardagullian,
High ground of holly tree,
        A stable door rattles in far off Bethlehem.
Our eyes, ears, mouth and nose are full of Christmas.

Flame of candles, crackle of log fire.
        Sprigs of berry-holly hide behind pictures
The tail-light of the postman's bicycle
        Slips past the gable
Aunt Annie has had too much sherry
        And is quarrelsome,
Aunt Gretta dips Christmas cake in her tea.

Our eardrums are full of Christmas toys
        Mouth organ, tin whistle, drums, a train set...
Tasty smells to tickle the palate: turkey, stuffing, plum pudding, whiskey...
        The two aunts are whispering in the hallway
Clink of glasses, Uncle Jack assures us:
        We've come through another Christmas - unscathed.
It's great to be alive.

Crossing-Out Christmas

Santa Claus nailed to
A Cross, in a shop window
Somewhere in Japan.

Song of a Sewing Machine

I am wellington deep
In the wet meadow in Granardkille.
Smell of yesterday's rain in the rushes,
A snipe removes her long bill
From the scabbard of her wing
To sing a sewing machine song:
Ja-Pa, Ja-Pa, Ja-Pa...
Then flies from tuft of rushes
Sky-spiralling,
Drifting,
Darting
Left Right
Her long snipe bill pierces open
Wounds of childhood memory,
The sky,
A hospital bed of clouds
Hangs above me
Aunt Gretta sinks her head in pillows
Grows striped feathers, darts from the clouds
Sky-spiralling down
To open the Iron Gate
That leads to Cronogue's Lane.

Something Lost

Something old, deep in the gut
Takes me outdoors tonight
To walk the roads.
Winter winds blow across
        A wilderness of fields.
The moon listens.
Bushes shiver in the snow,
Candle flames wink from farm windows
At a frightened child in the dark
And I long to reconnect
With something I've lost.

Rus in Urbe

The city was once a field
Before the mouldboards came
To turn it over
Into drills of smoking chimneys,
Headlands of High-Rise

All living together
Solitary lives
In cramped dens of bricks and blocks
Looking up at the stars, dreaming of fields
Before the mouldboards turned them over.

No More History, A Choral Ode

Strophe	<>	**Antistrophe**
We must try to forget		To remember, to remember
Losing our land,		Losing our language
All the big Houses		Separated by garden walls
All the botháns		Behind the ditch
We must try to forget		To remember, to remember
Catholics		Protestants
Workhouses		Bully's Acre
A man shot dead		District Inspector Kelleher
Shot dead		In the Greville Arms Hotel
Why are you leaving?		Where you are going?
Grid of border roads		Map of veins on Mrs. Brady's feet
Laundries		Industrial Schools
Keep the light bulb		Away from our darkness
Helicopters on the border		Barbed wire, plastic bullets
Bloody Sunday		Good Friday
Where two worlds		Come together
Didn't		Couldn't
No forbidden apples left		Women emigrated in droves
A halo away from history		All the forgotten times
Sitting in silence		Lost to blanket clouds in the sky
We are the children		Without History Class
Sir! What is the past?		Miss! What's a national anthem?
No more looking back		You must look forward
We are the children		Deprived of our

Rights to Remember.

Last Outpost to the Gods

Mainland.
How are you!
We are just another island,
                                        Cut off.

It's one Big Theatre of Cruelty Here.
Dia Mór   agus   dia beag
Who's holding the gun to God's head ?
Everything is becoming too hot
The lid won't stay on the pot
We need to save ourselves from ourselves
City streets full of open manholes.
No corncrakes, no curlews, few hares ...
All walking in someone else's shoes
Shouting for legal rights for robots.

All the rainy islands in the West
Spoke Irish and starved.
But the boot's on the other foot now:
No priest, no doctor, no Post Office,
No bar to drink or talk in
It's all down to the behaviour of words now.
As the priest once said on Inishmore:
Send us boats or send us coffins.

Meditation On Lough Oughter

Span of water,
scatter of islands,
Flood of light from the lake.
Attune yourself to a new rhythm,
Let the lake-water go through its motions,
The oar blades cut the steel-grey light,
Up and down of boats and cots
Ripple and popple of lake-water.

Let the lake-water throw light on the past,
Riddle-me-ree of history
Rise and fall of fortunes,
A Middle Age Commedia dell'Arte
de Lacy, Magnifico O'Reilly, il Capitano O'Rourke
Constantly juggling for power
All the spilt blood
At Clough Oughter Castle,
Bishop Bedell imprisoned there.

Further down on Trinity Island
Desolate, wild and lonely,
Monks in white habits
Sang *Laudes* to the faint light of dawn
Monks intent on growing halos,
Welcomed pilgrims and the poor,

Curve of limestone teeth
Above the door
Tangle and Twist
Curlicue and Squiggle
Of the stones
Nights of long silence
Cells lit by the stars.

Times change

They lost their patrons. It wasn't easy.
Mayhem and madness prevailed.
Local wars, famine, bubonic plague,
Weather bad and harvest late,
The ornate doorway to their church,
Snatched and lodged in Kilmore.
Unruliness in the order
Hunger for money and lust
A string of Stenterello Sheridans as Priors,
Bishops and Abbots dressed up as shepherds
Proctor Brady, with pockets full of tithes.

Lough Oughter is a different prayer now.
You can be alone with the silence and the swans.
Lough Oughter will tell you:
Who you were, who you are...
Shadows cross the lake-water,

There's that open invitation to search
The deep and dark abyss,
All the way down to the mudstones
And the first bones of fish.

The ruins of the castle and priory
Continue to swap stories
Ruins to endure
Like ghosts of tomorrow.

Cavan Singers

Founded 1984

A jubilant journey started,
When moon longed for the shimmer of morning
And days of woes at work were tiresome,
Semibreves, minims, crotchets, quavers
Spread across the Cavan Singers'pages
Life laughed and we became its story.

I return as a ghost now looking back
To Tuesday nights for rehearsals:
Stops and starts and scales .... sheet music
For our perusal, jubilant voices climbing higher
Jubilate Deo Omnis Terra

Choir contests in Wales & Rome ...
Voices raised to heaven pondering
Every note, enjoying each inflection
And the loyal support: husbands, wives
A sea of faces cheering on the Cavan Singers.

        Charity performances for one cause or another
Lines of parked cars outside the Parochial Hall,
Cups of tea, ham sandwiches half shy of mustard,
Talk and more talk ...

                Christmas Carol Singing
Outside the Post Office, Winter lanterns,
Sprigs of red-berried holly
In every overcoat, hat, and scarf
Memories sleep in peace now,
Sleep in heavenly peace....

The Cavan Singers' life-long desire
Was and is: To bring joy to all who listen
And to honour the memory of all departed members.
Let the final sentiments of "Va Pensiero"
Soften into silence:
So That We May Endure To The Last
May Endure To The Last.

Commemoration

Ballinamuck, 1798

It all happened in the long ago,
Weeks before we dug the potatoes.
There were rumours of liberation everywhere:
The French Are On Their Way.
Today we are left to remember
Ballinamuck and the ghosts of '98.

We recall the chaos of it all,
Clash of metal ringing out, soldiers shouting,
Cavalry charging,
The wounded shoving moss into their wounds
The dead and the dying
Abandoned in bog holes.

Listen:
Can you hear the hills shout their goodbyes?
Let the familiar place names ring in your ears:
Kiltycreevagh, Shanmullagh Hill,
Fearglass Lough, Dromgort,
Gaigue.

Pain still endures here
These fields continue to spark our memory,
Our hearts are filled with mixed emotions:
Love, fear, sadness, anger ...
Trees wail with the sorrow of rain,
Blackberries bleed on thorns.

Slow breath, last breath of the hanged and drowned
Bubble of bog water coming up from below
Underworld of prayers in Irish,
Old women gather round:
Sé do bheatha, a Mhuire,
Atá lán de ghrásta ...

Yet there is solace here.
Our heroes live on: The Gunner Magee,
General George Blake, Brave Robin Gill of Fardromin ...
Ballinamuck
Continues to connect with us
To inspire us.

It's a place to be creative,
A place drifting in and out
Of the rhymes and rhythms of fields,
A hare's corner
To endure
The withering winds of winter.

What Does Being Irish Mean To You Today?

Hanging on to the past for our dear lives
Forever plucking at the harp-strings of history,
Our language almost silenced
We sat brooding over the lost acres.
Yet freedom was always a light
Left on in our souls.

Unexpectedly,
All hell broke loose on the streets of Dublin.
The pent-up energy spread to the countryside
And a Treaty followed.

                    Hail to a weirdly wonderful gathering
In room 112 of the Shelbourne Hotel, Dublin
Riddle-me-ree of History
A new patriotism comes to life:
We have achieved at last the freedom
To determine:
                    Who we are
                    Where we come from
                    Where we are going

Dánta i nGaeilge agus Aistriúchain

Poems in Irish and Translation

Seisreach

Cuimhne m'athair ina chéachtaire,
Dhá chapall ag tarraingt
Céachta iarainn is rotha iarainn
Ag triall go mall le fána,
Is súile m'athair ghreamaithe
Ar sceach gheal taobh thíos de
Is an scór síor díreach aige
I bpáirc seimre chapaill, i gcónaí.

A Pair Of Plough Horses

I remember my father ploughing,
Two horses pulling
The iron plough and the iron wheel
Moving slowly down the hill,
And my father's eyes glued
To a white thorn bush below him
And he forever keeping a straight line
In the red clover field.

Smaointe Fánacha Ó Ghleannghaibhle

Cloisim diadhánach na bó
Ar an ngaoth,
Feicim cailleach ag crú trí chriathar,
Gamháin le gobán ar strae.

Ar bhealach na bó finne
Tá stóilín trí chos a gearradh sa chloch
Cois locha
        A ghlacann an spéir.

Stray Thoughts From Glangevlin

I hear on the wind
The lowing of a cow for her calf,
I see a hag milk into a sieve ,
A calf lost to a goban.

On the pathway of the white cow
Is a three-legged stool cut in stone
Beside the lake
        That holds the sky.

An Chailleach ó Lough an Leagh

Is mise an chailleach ó Lough an Leagh
Do chara ó bhreith go bás
Ag síor cogaint gairleoige
Mo phráiscín lán de giuirléidi
Eolas na treibhe im chuimhne
Banríon Óiríon um gheimhridh.

Ach! Ar theacht an earraigh
Bainim díom caille de sioc is sneachta
Athraím cruth:
Ó fheannóg dhubh go lasair coille
Ó bhean chríonna go cailín óg
I'm chráinbheach na maidine
Iomas gréine im shúile.

The Hag from Lough an Laogh

I'm the hag from Lough an Leagh
Your friend from cradle to grave
Forever chewing garlic
My apron full of knick-knacks
My memory with recall for the tribe.
I'm Queen Óiríon of winter nights.

But! When Spring arrives
I remove my shawl of frost and snow.
I metamorphose:
From hooded-crow to golden finch
From old age to youth
I'm the Queen bee of the morning
Eyes sparkling with sunlight..

An Créacht A Leigheas

I gcuimhne Béal Átha na Muc, 1798

Sheas siad an fód dúinn
Sheas siad gualainn ar ghualainn
Sheas siad dílis go bás
I bportach creatha

Fuineadh agus fáisceadh iad as an áit
Ar aon le naoscach, is crotach
Ar aon le cré leighis:
    Lus na fola
    Lus an Ghrá
    Lus na hOíche
    Lus an chodlata

To Heal The Wound

In memory of Ballinamuck,1798

They Stood up for us
They stood shoulder to shoulder
They stood faithful unto death
In a quaking bog

They were part of nature there
At one with the snipe and curlew ..
At one with the healing earth:
    Shepherd's purse
    Love-Lies- Bleeding
    Night Shade
    Poppy Sleep

Let the Images Unfold

Let The Images Unfold

Let the images unfold
Let them happen by chance
Let us walk with the moon child
There's no real plot here
        No agenda
                No border guard checking papers.

We are all fellow-travellers
On the streets tonight
        Celebrate with squeal, moo, hoot, and neigh
                Tell your secrets
                        To The Milky Way.

The Egg Market

I wonder what the Egg Market
Is hatching up?
A world of free range hens and turkey cocks
A world for our imagination
A world to live in
A world to remember.

We recall the Hen Woman
Her head in her sparán
Forever counting threepenny bits and tanners
And The Fleadh Cheoil Days
All the trad music, lepping and dancing
And Seán Ó Sé:
Ailliliú An Poc Ar Buile...

A Much-Travelled Image

Sheep drift in the moonlight
To walk about the town,
Behold the man, the shepherd,
He knows the wolves are just
Around the corner of every street.
The churches are very close to one another,
They can hear each other breathe.
The sheep are grazing
                    In a special space
Neither inside or truly outside.
Darkness speaks to the light:
Relics of memories haunt us
We hear the purr of prayer from within,
The congregation kneeling, sitting, standing...
All the timeless binding between nature and us.

Scapegoat

Blow the shofar
From Rosh Hashana to Yom Kippur,
Find an Old Testament goat to blame
Let him carry your shame
Hang all your sins on his horns
        Blame the goat, beat the goat
        Beat the beat, the oldest song
        Blame the goat, beat the goat
        Have him wipe your slate clean
Drag the goat to the desert sands
Leave him there to wither and die
To die and wither in the wilderness.

Street Galleries

Here we have animals
In familiar Cavan places,
All wired-up, paper-skinned, alight
And ready to go,
Prompting us to have thoughts:
        A lens to probe our memories
        Of fish bones locked in stone,
        The bitter winds, the sleet and snow
        That only the hills know.

Let's consider them for a moment
As animals in themselves,
Not just our human projections ...
        These are no soft toys.
Silence hangs about the streets
Listening to the rainfall.
They have all endured,
A museum of animals and birds
Forever caged in our words.

Abbeylands

This is High Status burial ground.
Here we have: trees, walls, grave stones
And the Bell-Tower
Alongside an installation of:
Cows, goats, fox and stag...
                    Hare, cat and donkey...
This is St. Mary's Abbey
Franciscan Friary, Cavan
Burnt down many's the time
        By a friar drunk on wine,
                By John Tiptof, the Sasanach
                        And by O'Reilly's wife, Mad Mary.

Maynooth Calling

Maynooth Calling

Route 66

We gathered at the Quays in Dublin, awaiting the bus. Route 66 travelled through Lucan, Leixlip and final destination was Maynooth. Many of us were making the journey for the first time and we stared at the leaves floating down the river Liffey rather than make eye contact with each other. The 66 bus finally arrived and we stacked our big cases in the luggage compartment. An elderly lady complained to the driver:

Them young fellows going to be priests are holding us all up.

We hailed from all corners of Ireland, from the drumlins of Cavan and Monaghan, the dry stone walls of Mayo and Galway. Students from Derry seemed to know each other and had more to say. The babble of different accents from different dioceses was confusing. By the time the bus reached Leixlip we had settled down and some of us began to talk about the little events in our lives: the schools we attended, football matches, a book or two one enjoyed reading. This time the bus went all the way up to the gates of the college, a special favour by C.I.E. We dragged our cases past the Geraldine Castle and walked in the direction of Stoyte House. We were met and welcomed by senior clerics. Friendly faces asked reasonable questions:

And your name is?

And your diocese?

A litany of diocesan place names ensued: Kilmore, Clogher, Ossory, Ardagh and Clonmacnoise ...

Take a left and you'll arrive at Rhetoric House. You can't miss it.

It's the building with red ivy climbing the walls. You'll be told more there.

The whole place seemed enormous. On the outside it was larger than any village, more the size of a country town with chapels and squares and houses. Huge blocks of houses: Stoyte House, Logic House, Dunboyne House, Rhetoric House, New House... These great buildings lay between beautifully manicured garden squares. We strolled through a garden of rose climbers and flowering shrubs behind Logic House, safe in the imaginative world of our newly found vocation. It all seemed like Eden that evening.

After supper we were summoned to the chapel. We sat there in silence. Homesickness was beginning to strike for the first time. The Junior Dean congratulated us on our undertaking of a difficult journey in life. He talked about detachment from home, how we must face the loneliness and separation. But he assured us we were not entering this world all by ourselves. Our Guardian Angels were guiding us there. We were the chosen few.

The routine began the following morning. The Gun Bell rang out a six o'clock call.

Maynooth Calling

Was a world of bells and bell talk:
Bells for the waking
                    Bells to raise you up
Jubilant bells
                    Faint bells
Bells to impress upon your mind
                    Mystery bells
                            Evangelical bells
Bells to tell you:
God is well and   So are you ...

Bloody bells, you have a habit of repeating yourselves
Can't you see I'm not well
I'm truly going mad
As mad as mad Nebuchadnezzar
Eating grass for seven years in some remote field in the bible.

Protected by Big Walls

Bleary eyed, we made our way to The Junior Chapel for Laudes, a morning hymn of praise.

It wasn't all prayer. Each diocese had a gathering space called a " Pause". Here we were given tips on survival tactics by Senior Clerics. We soon became fluent in the inside lingo: "*Chubs*", "*Logs*" and "*BÁs*" – 1st Years, 2nd Years, and BA students. And there were other novelties. We were wearing our priestly garments for the first time. Our days were full of swinging thuribles, candle-light and Gregorian chant. It was all consuming. A way of life that had instant appeal for us but it was early days yet.

And there was academic excitement about studying for an arts degree. The College had a lively creative atmosphere. We had a Literary and Debating Society, a Philosophical Society... I saw a student production of Beckett's "Waiting For Godot" in The Aula Maxima.

And the canonical figures of literature awaited us: Kierkegaard, Heidegger, Sartre and Camus...

But all the initial excitement slowly faded. Each evening hidden away in my room I had time to reflect. The community life was losing its hold on me. I was beginning to question a world of posturing for the priesthood. Listening to the trains passing in the night I pondered the big questions: Did I really want to take up residence in some parochial house in some remote parish? What was really calling me? Was I in search of instant respectability and a steady job? Was I a chosen one?

Maynooth was a safe house to rest in after the Leaving Certificate. Everything was provided for us. We had the best of food. We were protected by big walls from the outside world. We wore birettas for helmets and deadly black soutanes. We were training to become princes of the church. We played croquet on the front lawn.

Outside Rhetoric House

Clerics stand about the front door of Rhetoric House talking, smoking and in short putting in time. It is an opportunity for a smoke after breakfast, a smoke in between lectures, in between bouts of study in the Junior library. The usual suspects never fail to turn up and torment one another. A log from the diocese of Meath has a reputation for bumming a cigarette:

Any chance of a Cigarette?

Me tongue is always out for one after breakfast.

You're a Godsend.

Are you the chub from Kilmore Diocese that belongs to an Abbey?

I am

What abbey is that?

Kilnacrott. I'm a Premonstratensian.

Holy God... That's something to be proud of ... a Pre ... what?

A Premonstratensian

And they let you smoke?

Yes.

Well fair play to them, them Pre ...Pre –mons-trat-en-sians. Hey Pat Joe, come over here.

Did ya meet this chub from Kilmore? Tell Pat Joe what ya are.

He knows me. We often meet for a smoke outside Rhetoric.

I was only joking. Pre-mons-tra-ten-sians.

God knows. We all need to be humbled before God

Tanderagee Down On One Knee!

Maynooth is a factory for the priesthood in Ireland. Too many priests.

They don't want half of us. They're saying we'll have to go to England

For the first few years and wait for a curacy to fall vacant back home.

You have to be talking about something. Don't ya Pat Joe?

I was at my first lecture yesterday:

God Is and God Is Not

This Is Me and This Is Not Me

We need to make up our minds about religion.

(He throws away the butt)

Good morning to you gentlemen.

The Gunn Chapel, Maynooth

Rose window of calm and peace colours
Catch the curve of morning

Soutane and surplice
Fill the carved oak stalls

Faces shift heavenwards
To pray the songs of the prophets

Laus Deo,   *Praise God,*
Praise wild plants, birds and animals:

Lambs bleating   Across at each other
Heaven and earth   Talking to each other
Swells and eddies of rhythms and sounds
        Domine exaudi orationem meam
        Et clamor meus ad te veniat

White faces longing for breakfast
Dreaming of milk on cornflakes
And the first drag of a *Sweet Afton* cigarette,
Outside Rhetoric House.

Sometimes, I felt pampered there. Surrounded by quiet and peacefulness, I longed for the irreverence of youth. I needed to break free and find excitement in a world where anything and everything happens. I longed for a world of t-shirts and jeans. I imagined myself with a rucksack and guitar heading for Route 66 again. But this time it would take me to Los Angeles, the city of angels.

When the Girls Arrived

That's logic house just in front of you.

The clerics outside will get your brother for you.

A chorus of: *Thanks very much*, from the girls.

I arrive down at the door of Logic House to greet my sister Geraldine and two other girls: Lily from Kerry and Thomasina from Donegal. All taking a commercial course in Loreto, Crumlin. The girls arrived unexpectedly. They were striking. Three tall figures. Faces alight like angels come down to earth. They create a stir outside Logic House. Jim Brady, a cleric said:

They're an instant cure for my pounding headache

John inquires:

Where did you find the Marilyn Monroes?

Thomasina laughs:

Aren't you going to invite us up to see your room?
We're not supposed to bring anyone up to our room.
Suppose nothing much wrong with it? Come on then...

Our voices are down to whispers going up the stairs. All six of us squeeze into the cell room no. 59. The door clicks shut. A Spartan place, grey flannel curtains.

Pull the curtain there Jim in case the clerics on the Desert will be able to see in.

Each of us stands apart. Almost afraid, we hardly know what to say or do. Lily runs her hand through her hair. Her hair falls in waves like sea grass. Suddenly the room smells fresh and exotic and the girls' perfume permeates everywhere. Lily said her perfume:

Comes from something secreted from a sperm whale

We are all uncomfortable and all too close to one another. We are little more than shapes and colours in the dim light. Lily's green cap floating, Geraldine's Sunday coat shimmering, Thomasina's kilt shifting ...

Gradually, we became ghostly figures, talking to ourselves, no one really listening, no one really answering ... We stepped in and out of conversations. A pattern of questions followed from the girls:

How do you clerics put in the time?

Is celibacy absolutely necessary?

Has Lourdes any Holy Water left?

What keeps ya here?

Then a great silence awaited the answers. A silence you hear before Bruckner's *Locus iste ad Deo factus est:*

John said: *Elohim, who is The Living God keeps me here.*

Oh! Jesus! Sorry I asked. Hello Him, Hello Him... How are Ya Doing?

To break a deadly silence, Geraldine goes over to the book case and takes a book from the shelf, wets her thumb and fingers through the pages.

What's this book about?

That's Latin poetry, Ars Amatoria by Ovid.   *The Art of Love.*

Is this your school book?

Yes. It's on for First Arts. Ovid is one of the Augustan poets.

It's about how women should walk and dance and laugh... You know, to retain a lover's affection

So that's what you clerics are been taught here.

Thomasina teases:

I forgot my castanets, otherwise I'd dance a flamenco for you all.

Who would believe it? Women learn to laugh according to Ovid.

What about singing?

They learn to sing also: *Discant cantare puellae*   *Girls learn to sing.*

God! We're in the wrong place,

We should be out here learning how to become proper women

Do you have a spare room?

We could always stay in the wardrobe for the night

Noises creep in from outside: A loud cheer from the Desert. Someone has scored a goal. The conversation stops and starts on this dreamy Sunday afternoon. Geraldine grabs me by the arm to say:

Be sure to write to Mom! Won't you now!

You could tell the other girls were losing interest in our way of life, our snippets of Latin poetry and they slip quietly out of the room, down the stairs and away with them to catch a bus to Dublin.

A Group of Students, Birettas On, Stand Like Statues, Facing Heaven

(strophe	**antistrophe)**	(spoken as if in choir)
Long corridors	many doors,	
God took us here	or did He?	
To be marked out	a chosen one	
Took our names	assigned us numbers instead	
All searching	for something lost	
Loved by our mothers	Pueri Aeterni	
Word in the womb	the word made flesh	
Converting myths	into day-to-day living	
Carrying our heads	in our hands	
Seminarians	behind a high wall	
Seminarians	A seed sowing race	
Inside the	Pomerium	
Bells toll	you are only a number	
The holy rood	fish on Fridays	
Rules are rules	auto-da-fé	
Birettas in our hands	birettas on our heads	
Better reign in heaven	than burn in hell.	

The Kildare Chubs

A hushed silence in Callan Hall.
They were introduced as: The Kildare Chubs,
Chubs were first year students in the seminary,
Winged angelic beings, chubby-healthy fellows
Or so the rest claimed.
The Kildare Chubs could take us out of ourselves

If only for the length of a song or two.
They lifted Callan Hall and the empty day,
Their voices soared
With shafts of light and freedom:
Familiar phrases from the songs:
    We are freeborn men of the travelling people,
    Got no fixed abode of nomads we are numbered ...
And their signature tune:
    And it's then I will repair to the Curragh of Kildare,
    For it's there I'll find tidings of my dear ...
Then the Razz, excitement, and applause
And slowly
Each returned to his cell and himself for the night.

Photos Hang on the Walls

Faces on the wall,
Clerics like mice smiling
Look down at us,
We look up with curiosity.
        We look up at them.
        With Fantasies about their faces.
        Reading into their lives
Dressy fellows in soutanes
Faces about to make the sign of the cross,
Faces about to sing a *Hymn to Mary,*
*Up The Catholi*c faces

Praise the Lord faces.
Laus Deo
Fleur- de- lis faces.
        Lines of faces in carved oak stalls,
        Rotatory faces in the dust grains of sunlight,
A face attached to suffering,
A face with a poem on its lips
        Ethereal faces,
        Gravitational faces,
        Faces singing from the same hymn sheet,
A rose window is caught in a curve of light,
A thurible sends smoke down the aisle,
A white surplice dances in the draught of an open door.

Nuns

And there was an invasion of nuns in Maynooth in the 70s.
Nuns of a feather pray together
Nuns of a feather laugh together
Nuns of a feather stay together
Sisters of Mercy, Sisters of the Poor Shepherd, Sisters with Arts Degrees,
Nuns with secrets up their sleeves,
Nuns with ropes round their waists and three knots hanging,
A bare-faced Mother Superior, God between us and all harm,
Sisters to darn the priests' socks,
Nuns from Dublin jigging up the avenue,
Sister Cup and Sister Saucer, put the kettle on,

Mother Godiva put your habit on,
A flutter of nuns looking at the night sky and the whereabouts of heaven...
A flutter of nuns discussing the merits of nuns
Nuns reciting three decades of the rosary for the repose of the soul of
Dannyboy ...
Oh! Dannyboy, Pray For Us, Pray For Us ...

Day Out in Dublin

It was Sunday. A day out in Dublin. The bus stopped at Bachelor's Walk.
This bus will leave Aston Quay at 6.30 promptly.
It's just across the river Liffey there.
I won't wait for anyone, the driver said.
We disembarked. All in our black suits, white shirts, black ties.
Some of us carried umbrellas and those who wished to be liturgically complete
Wore black hats. We were all self conscious of our sacerdotal plight
Of black and white. A woman on O'Connell Street stopped to ask us:
Are ye going to be priests or parsons?
And she enjoyed her joke and went off laughing to herself.
We were now street walkers for the day.
Some of us met our sisters in Wynn's Hotel,
Ate buns, drank coffee in a haze of cigarette smoke
And talked about life back at home.
The Divinity Students were more upmarket
And dined in The Gresham where napkins
Were mitres for the day,
Others went to the cinema, "The Ambassador"
Showing: *Oliver*, the musical.
We were constantly running into one another
In clusters of threes and fours
Walking and talking and putting in the time.
Back on the bus
Garry, a divinity student was groggy,
The colour of death and he threw up
And the bus driver made him clean up.

Curse of the Ghost Room

Maynooth College

What hound from hell barked
In their ears?
What devil drove them astray?
That they should slit their throats
From ear to ear,
Rust of blood on the floor boards
Behaviour beyond the loop of logic,
Compelled by some demonic force
They threw themselves out the window
Of Room 2, upper floor,
Rhetoric House, Maynooth.

All born the same way
Yet we die different deaths.

Trees line the avenue
        To the college cemetery,
The tragic clerics lie buried here
In graves beyond
                The consecrated plot.
Room No. 2 is now an oratory.
Dedicated to Saint Joseph,
Patron of peaceful deaths
Rumours continue to grow and spread
Words have wings.

Logic House

My room in Logic House is tiny.
There are few surprises there,
The sun rises, the sun sets.
A crucifix hangs above my bed,
There's a wardrobe and a book shelf.
A few books lean against one another:
The Bible, "At Swim Two Birds", a book
To assassinate the novel
        or so the wiser seminarians say and
"Mo Bhealach Féin, I love that book:
Is óg i mo shaol a chonaic mé uaim é,
An ród sin a bhí le mo mhian ...
But what on earth am I facing?
What road lies before me?

And another book, I almost forgot:
My mother's prayer book.
Every evening we are left to a world of study, thought...
Watching the play of shadows.
You can hear the dusk and darkness coming,
A long train sighs past in the distance.
Philosophy is difficult,
                Hard to concentrate on abstract thoughts
A mind wanders easily, dreaming of playing
With church toys: Monstrance, Pyx, Chalice, Pattens...
Dressing up in costume: Alb, Cincture, Chasaubile ...
A vocation for the social elite: *I Have Chosen You*.

Has God anything new to say this evening?
The window looks out on The Desert,
A playing field of scorched earth for soccer.
The copper beach is standing at the corner
Logic House has many rooms.
On the ground floor to the right
You have the Chemistry lab. with glugger smells

Seeping up to all our rooms
Here the Dom. presides,
A Dominican Friar, Professor of Chemistry
With an insatiable appetite to give sermons
In honour of the Blessed Virgin Mary.

You can almost sense the end of study confinement.
Chairs in other rooms scrape the floor boards.
Doors start opening, voices are heard in the corridor
Everyone is heading to the Junior Refectory in Rhetoric House.

The Garden

Every now and then I love to sit in the garden
Behind Logic House.
I long to reconnect with something.
It's my Eden, my Gethsemane,
Two sides of myself
At odds with each other.
Flowerbeds of sweet peas, supported on bamboo canes
Lie to my right,
Sweet William attracts the bees,
Montbretia and Ox Eye Dasies lean against a wall,
There's a ladybird , bóín Dé on a rose.
A sundial stands off centre,
A rockery of small flowers and stones on my left.
The gardener is somewhere close,
Toil and till ...
A rake and shovel lie in his wheelbarrow.
Flurry of leaves, flurry of ideas,
I love to daydream, ponder time away...
        When will this garden revert back to chaos?
When it's left alone.
        Cultivation, civilization are man made?
Vatican 2? The Age of Aquarius,
        A time when nobody is listening to anybody.
Time passes more slowly for your feet than your head!
A bell rings.

A FLAME

A Flame was an outdoor party particular to the clerical students in Maynooth. It happened when the exam season was over and students were about to go on the long summer holidays. The weather was usually good, plenty of sunshine and students were ready to let their hair down a little:

We sat around on our posteriors in the grass,
Drank fizzy drinks from plastic cups,
Ate plates of sandwiches:
Ham, cheese, egg salad, salmon...
Followed by: cakes, buns, apple tarts ...
Throughout we entertained one another
Telling clerical jokes:

Did ya hear the one about the two Jesuits?
There was this parish priest who was having a mission
And he got two of the finest preaching Jesuits down

To put the fear of God into the parishioners .
Lo and behold... when the mission was over
The Parish Priest had two of his finest pullets choked
And cooked and served up to the Jesuits for dinner.
When they were all sitting down to the dinner
The cock outside began to crow louder than ever before?
What's that cock crowing about one Jesuit inquired?
And the Parish Priest Answered:
Doesn't he know he has two sons in the Jesuits.

Ha –Ha-Ha-Ha –Ha ...

Some fell over in the grass with the laughing.
That's a good one. I think I heard that one last year.

To break the monotony of clerical jokes
Others strummed guitars and sang:

Kum Ba Yah My Lord
Kum Ba Yah
Kum Ba Yah My Lord

Kum Ba Yah...
That was a song that refused to end:
Someone's singing Lord ...
Someone's crying Lord ...
And like the flame itself the song had no end ...

Bind Us Together

Outside, night stretches around us. Different dioceses meet for what is termed *A Pause*, in Maynooth terminology. It's a way to enable students to stay together:

a ritual, a collective conversation, a circle of heads and shoulders wedged together, nodding, glancing this way and that, shifting from one foot to another one seminarian fiddles with his soutane buttons,

Another is blowing into his hands and complaining about the cold in September.

Practically everyone is smoking cigarettes, lighting cigarettes with great ceremony and blowing smoke into the night like it was a liturgy all to itself. Only one stony-faced cleric puffs away at his pipe and asks:

What will we talk about?

Heads turn together Heads turn away:

Several topics come up for discussion:

The Common Room and Newspapers, the soccer league, how are the Chubs settling in? Life back in the Diocese of Kilmore ... the play coming up in the Aula Maxima ...

One gives a blow-by-blow account of some local football game.

Someone is criticizing another student for over-baking for exams,

Can't take his head out of the books.

Another is mimicking a Maths Teacher he once had in St. Patrick's College,

A chub, a new kid on the block,

Talks of becoming a bishop:

But deep down, he means it.

I'd love to wear a zucchetto

I'm only joking...

Some are silent, unable to get a word in edgeways.

A fourth Divinity Student playing the older and wiser tells us about: Hans Kung, a modern theologian.

Downcast heads hear the story,

Heads uplift for the laugh: *Ha ,Ha, Ha,...*

Someone asks a question:

Talking without boasting,

Why does God want us to believe in Him?

A pause in the pause

A third Divinity Student advises all:

Let's not indulge ourselves,

We have to get away from the middle ages,

Princes of the church and all that

Conceited clerics in full regalia

Table napkins and silver rings at table,

Read Michel Quoist's : Prayers of Life

He'll bring us all down to earth...

A train passes almost touching the trees in the distance.

Rain Beats Against My Bedroom Window

Rain beats against my bedroom window in Logic House. Another night train is shunting past in my sleep, beyond the darkness of trees, past fields and hedgerows of sleep,

Who, who, who, shush... who, who, who, shush...

Shuddering throb of the train...

Loud at first, then pushing its way into silence,

Arriving in dreamland:

The people that walked in darkness have seen a great light.

Train of thoughts in your sleep

Walk in the light of God...

A procession of soutanes walk past Rhetoric House, Logic House.

Bishops with a lot on their minds saunter around St. Joseph's Square.

Where are they heading? Where am I heading?

What's bothering them:

Falling number of clerics?

Lay Students in Maynooth?

Humanae Vitae?...

Every issue keeps building up, annoying you, takes a lot out of you, a draining sickness sucks life from your bones, all that reflection night after night, all the doubts...

Clerics not really needed anymore? But who will build the hospitals? Clinics? Schools?

We no longer need an army of Black Anoraks.

The laity will do it all now.

Our real purpose in life lies hidden to us all. It's one big mystery.

It always was and will be one big mystery

Get out while the going is good, become a lay student, get a degree, get a job and get married like the rest. You haven't a calling. You only imagined it. Cutting is a lonely business. Don't wait till Christmas.

Go Now. Now, Now, Now...

Land of Nod

Night after night of late,
I travel to the Land of Nod in my sleep.
I hear many voices:
The devil is up to his tricks, luring me away.
My angel Guardian tries to soothe my soul to sleep,
I am constantly moving and shuffling...
I know I am keeping my distance away from the rest.
On my own and I know it,
Carrying my head in my hands.
God has become distant.
God isn't a person
God isn't even a thing to me now.
When I awaken it is still the same
I stay away from Mass in the morning.
I seldom answer:
Morning bells, day bells, evening bells,
My fellow students are shocked
To see me read The Communist Manifesto
The odd time I turn in for meditation.
Go Now, Now, Now, Now ...

Home I Come Again

It was triumphal.
Verdi's : Grand March from Aida
Played on the organ after vespers
When a seminarian was about to cut.

It never failed to move us all.
Some knew who it was.

Others spend the evening trying to find out.

Who is going to "cut"?
"Cut". Maynooth terminology
For abandoning ship.

The trumpet voluntary gave a sense of occasion.
He had fought the good fight.
Every Seminarian was suspect
Who showed signs of:
Crankiness?
            Excitability?
                        Borderline Insanity?
I hadn't a true vocation.
Only thought I heard the voice of God
In the thunder in Granardkille.
It was never like Moses' call from the burning bush.
It's back home for me. Back to the inland town.
Away with me now
With limited knowledge:
I know something of the Geography of hell
Can name some of its rivers:
Styx, Lethe, Tartarus...
Put to sleep now your dreams of Ordination Day.
The chance of you ever becoming a Bishop? An Abbot?

The junior Dean Bill Cos. Was understanding.

You want to leave. We won't stand in your way.
Have you a day in mind?
Wednesday Dr. Cosgrove.
Wednesday is good. Then Wednesday it is.
You will leave quietly. No fuss.
Have your people collect you outside Logic House at 7.10 am.
While the rest are at morning meditation,
Be sure to take all your belongings ...
God save you.

Wednesday morning arrived.
I waited at the door of Logic House with my suitcase and belongings.
One student was permitted to wait with me and keep me company.
He was all embarrassed and kept asking questions:
Who's collecting you?
How far is it from Maynooth to Granard?
You'll be home in two hours ... No more singing hymns to heaven for you...
A blue Ford Cortina passed Rhetoric House and headed for Logic House.
The headlights cut through a cold November morning.
My brother Richard had arrived to take me home.
I shook hands with Paddy Doherty, the student who kept me company.
Thanks Paddy, Thanks a million for waiting ... Keep the faith ... Goodbye now ...
It was a strange feeling leaving Maynooth that morning: All the clouds of doubt hadn't lifted.
A feeling like the gates of paradise had slammed shut behind me.
Why did you have to leave so early, my brother inquired.

Delivering Furniture

Late in November the wind talked to the rain. I was offered a job as a helper delivering furniture. The driver was a friend of mine and a nephew of the man who owned the furniture shop. I felt they all took pity on me. Wanted to help me get a grip back on life.

Poor fucker, home from the seminary and nothing to do!

We delivered to places like: Killasona, Lismacaffery, Boherquill ...

Off in the van smoking like troopers. There was a sense of freedom about it all. Up side roads, through fields, opening gates to reach remote houses, outdoor lights on in the yard, the dog barking, small children gather around the van to see what's happening. We lift a span new setee from the van, sideways through the door,

Be careful now!

Down a hallway to the sitting room.

The usual conversation and greetings:

You won't find Christmas now, less than three weeks left.

Is Santa coming to all these children?

Another delivery of nine chairs and three tables to a pub in Lismacaffery and Thomas reminds me to be quiet as the proprietor has had a bereavement and the month's mind was only yesterday.

Sorry time coming up to Christmas

I know that, your uncle Stephen was at the funeral.

Who's this man with you?

Ah1 he's just helping me, he broke out of the seminary a week ago

Where were you?

Maynooth.

Better go now than later.

Then he poured two large whiskeys

Get them inside you. It's a frosty morning.

We drank the whiskey neat and I spluttered by way out of the lounge bar to the great excitement of all. Back in the van we laugh at the madness of it all. Neat whiskey at eleven o'clock in the morning.

The Station House

The Station House was red-bricked and mobile and moved when trains passed day and night. It was to be my new residence as a lay student in the college. It took a bit of getting used to. It was a shelter for our external world as external students. It was a house of probability and chance happenings. Students called at different times for different reasons: For a cup of coffee and a chat, to borrow a text book, to extend the drinking hours after The Roost Bar, Brady's or Caulfield's closed. We chuckled over poems we had written, drew up a menu for Sunday dinner to offer the three New American girls:

American girls studying philosophy at their leisure, in Maynooth.

American girls, heart-throbs of all the male population, both clerical and secular

American girls who knew where their erogenous zones lay

American girls waiting and willing and we invited them in.

We were all one big family that Sunday afternoon as we sat about the kitchen table discussing Solipsism, Scepticism, Ireland's mental weather and all the rain, the harmonies of colours in the Renaissance and Gloria's paintings on the wall.

The Sunday cut was brisket, a chunk of beef that required at least four hours cooking. But we didn't know that and the American girls sat at table with a work ethic of:

Chewing,   Chawing   Masticating.

It was a time-consuming exercise their jaws will not forget

It was an embarrassment we could read in their terrible smiles.

The boys from Derry had scholarships and the British government helped pay for their rent. The rest of us from the South had to have our parents pay. So we had to deal with budgets for rent, food, electricity... It was a drama of existence and we were players and spectators at the one time: We discovered many aspects of the oneself:

"Is mó mé i mise", "There's many a me in myself"

Conor sits on the bed and sings from his song book: O Sole Mia ... then Edith Piaf: "No Regrets", *Non, Je Ne Regrette ...*

Sean has a heated discussion on the topic of "Free Derry & London Derry".

Joe Joe is hoping to marry a girl like his mother or so he says. But Joe Joe has issues and is hearing voices. He was away for a while and now that he's back, he walks about the college smiling to himself and showing his new fountain pen to anyone who bothers to stop to talk to him. Poor Fellow! We all feel self-conscious at times and Maynooth College is no different to anywhere else and all heads turn on swivels .

We all wear masks...

We can be crude and clumsy

We all laugh together

It all seems innocent when it's happening!

S-DRAP

Society for Disaffiliation, Reorientation of Agnosticated Peripatetics

It was a way of disguise, a war that cannot be waged in the open. Being truthful, we felt like misfits at the beginning. We formed a secret society, S-DRAP: A Society for Disaffiliated, Reorientation of Agnosticated Peripatetics. It was a mouthful. We had elevated thoughts and we frequented our rendezvous , the College Coffee Shop. We were epicurean, given to simple pleasures: drinking cups of coffee, eating buns and smoking like troopers. The Coffee Shop was a place to act out our fears for the future. The five of us were Cuts, clerics who abandoned the seminary and were now outside hoping to finish our studies as lay students. We were uneasy souls, uncertain somethings with a desire to philosophize:

When you exist you are not dead,

When you are dead you don't exist.

With serious cause and effect faces, we made logical advances to find the real truth about life. We rubbed our foreheads, rubbed our eyes with our fingers. We moved our arms, moved our legs in red armchairs, we opened our ears, sniffed with our noses for the scent of finding truth. We embraced being lay persons again. We eyed the eye-catching girls who were amused by our antics. We needed to speak to them but words were slow to come to us and when they did they were out of kilter:

O Sancta Simplicitas!

Who loves Petit Fait?

The Coffee Shop was a place to hang out in:

To wear a mask in

To make advances

To speak about yourself

To mouth words to girls

To rhapsodize the dainty ones

To laugh out loud and be proud

To be a member of S-DRAP,

A secret society of wonderment,

And questionable questions.

A Smack of Words on Your Tongue

Whoso, whereby words can change
By an by and will again
Clocks go back, clocks go on
By and by and will again.
Utopia   Distopia Retrotopia
Whoso, whereby life can change
Fields aflooding, roads aflooding, homes aflooding
By and by and will again
Wind Turbines   Christ on Calvary
Whoso, whereby life can change
Johnny begat Tommie begat Willie begat Seán Óg ...
By and by and will again
Somewhere, sometime all things end
Whoso, whereby life can end
Loss of breath, nervous cough and choke
Now he and she and we

Unhappy at home as the day is long
Morning, noon and night,
With a taste for words on our tongues.

Passage to America

The Ulster Bank gave me a loan to go to America, get summer employment and return and pay for the remainder of my education:
Summer in New York
Was forever in rush hour:
Turnstiles twisting, tickets slipping into slots...
Escalators going up and down,
Trains full of : eyes, ears, noses, mouths,
Sitting and standing, holding onto leather straps,
Silver bars, whatever they could grab hold of.
        I squeezed underneath
        A woman's hairy armpit,
        Droplets of silver sweat poured down,
        To distract my plight
        I started to count the seashells on her necklace,
        Eleven, twelve, fifteen, twenty one...
Never make eye contact on a train.
That's what everyone says.
Another train passes at high speed
Carriage lights flick on and off in flashes,
The train whistles into a Downtown Station.
Engine throbbing, doors open
A procession of people ascends the underworld
Heading up to streets of sirens, avenue buildings
That attack the sky.
Steel wire and suspension bridge,
Six lanes of roadway.

New York Never Sleeps:
It's all go on 42nd. Street:
I walk with my head down
Past a hippie singing: *Let the sunshine in*,
Someone else is
Sipping herbal tea and talking about polarity.
Sex Toy Shops and erotica everywhere,
Pussy cat pink music, peepshows

Bedroom candy and inflatable women ...
A child looks on eating a hot dog,
Tower blocks and apartments are falling asleep
In the midday sun, the pavement is thirsty.
Night Time
A fire burns in a brazier down a backstreet,
A man with sun glasses is sitting in a rocking chair,
Someone is eating out of a biscuit tin
Feet stick out of a barrel on its belly
More live in cardboard boxes
A ghetto-Blaster
Sings them asleep.

Mad On God

As soon as I left the clerics
A wild spirit grew inside me.
It was a time of rapture and terror.
Regular life and routine disappeared.
I became a louder shouter, slept in, missed lectures,
All the sorrowing eyes of the other clerics were on me.
Joe Joe stands motionless, staring into space:
When you have been mad on God
It's always difficult to quit Him.
Anyways. I wanted to break loose.
I had enough of hymn singing.
I wanted to write songs
With a dash of madness
About women throwing their heads back
Their hair flowing in the wind,
Beer gushing into the glass
Wild uproar, dazed smiles and the mad dance...
Wine and beer excites the madness
I dreamt I saw three girls
Bathe in lake water
And I a scarecrow in the oats field
Saw them coming up the hill
Carrying wine jars and figs to me
And I imbibed the vine
A goat dipped his beard in the river
And the ass had a mid-summer night's dream.

Summer in USA

It was the dawning of the Age of Aquarius
Free expression, free love...
The bars were full of students who opposed the war
Dylan's voice was everywhere
The Times They Are A Chang'in
Joan Baez: *We Shall Overcome*
I had a summer job
With Royal Doulton Minton Porcelain
Packing china plates and figurines
Antique English ceramics
Into the inner emptiness of a cardboard box
In a New Jersey Warehouse
From day to day
For one hundred dollars a week.
It was a summer born of lightning and strangely different.
I loved the chaos of the bars at night.
All the intoxicated delights
All the mortal women excited madness in me.
Their dazed smiles, their heads thrown back
Toss of their hair, blazing dance of lights
Till two or three in the morning...

Leonard Cohen's Music

When I returned to Maynooth in September I started to imitate the sounds and images of Leonard Cohen's songs. He was refreshingly new to me. Up to this I only knew Country Music and the lyrics were terrible, simplistic and over sentimental... all about "Gentle Mother"...

I loved Cohen's song: "So Long, Marianne".

Sounds and images went: *Kneeling through the dark.*

I was beginning to dream up something entirely new in music. I loved the light and darkness of it all. His lyrics were coloured differently. It was a new language, a new thinking in images:

You held on to me like I was a crucifix,

As we went kneeling through the dark...

It was a religion of passion, slow and sleepy at the start but building up to a climax. Forever free-thinking and free-spirited. It was soul-saving and just at the right time and over and over again I sang the Chorus and strummed chords in my bedroom in the Station House:

> *Now so long Marianne, it's time we*
>
> *Began*
>
> *To laugh and cry and cry and laugh*
>
> *About it all again ...*

Courtship in a Graveyard

Early spring. Before the exam pressure set in, Gloria and myself loved to escape the campus and take long walks into the countryside. Once we walked as far as Clongowes Wood College where Joyce was once a boarder. On another walk we came across a country graveyard and couldn't resist the temptation to slip inside and take refuge behind a headstone. It was so quiet, no one to disturb us. We had the place all to ourselves, an ideal spot for midday courtship if you were up for it. Gloria loved the sound of her own voice and she started to recite lines from the play "The Maids" by Janet. She was rehearsing the play in the College due to be staged in a couple of weeks. She stood in the calm stillness of the graveyard and gave a host of headstones a blast. She walked on tip-toe as if on stage.

What's the play about anyways?

Oh! It's about two maids, two sisters: Claire and Solange,
working for Madame. You won't like it. I know you won't.

The graveyard is hardly the place to rehearse

A graveyard is hardly a place for courtship, you don't object there.
Come to think of it, the graveyard is an ideal place,
Like Madame's bedroom where the play is meant to take place.
A bedroom or a graveyard, much of a muchness
You find flowers in both
Most of us are born in bed and die in bed.

What do you do in the play?

I have to undress.

Go ahead. This audience here won't mind and I'm easy

Madame will wear the white dress?
Madame will wear the red dress?
Put on your jewelry and makeup ...

Suddenly.Gloria spat.

Why did you do that?

> *"My jet of spit is my spray of diamonds"*
> *You think you can deprive me of the beauty of the sky*
> *Hah! Hah! Hah! Hah!...*

I'm out of here. You're goin' Fucken Mad
You're embarrassing the dead and me.
Time for us to get back to some sense of reality. Do some revision ...

I sat the BA examination the year the women in Dublin took the train to Belfast for the contraceptive pills and came back with aspirins ... I'll always remember getting the results back home and running down the fields in the lower reaches of Granardkille to tell my father and brother:

I passed.

The relief was enormous. I had something achieved at last:

I passed.

That September I started teaching in the local secondary school with H. Dip. Hours. I was commuting to Maynooth in the evenings for lectures. Maynooth continued to call.

H. Dip. Exams

I was sitting the H. Dip. Exams and I had no place to stay
No money to pay.
Terry Tully, a cleric came to my rescue.
Can't you stay in a room in Divinity,
A 4th. Year Divinity cut last week, you can stay in his room.
You can wear his soutane, he left it on the bed
Keep your head down, no one will tell
Be sure to turn off the lights, you know the game,
You were here before.
We'll bring you down for meals
Just keep eating and say nothing ...

It'll be grand !
Here's a transistor radio in case you get lonely.

It's all a hymn in my memory now, rolling out the mattress.
Sleeping in a forbidden place.
Turning off the light, listening to Radio Luxemburg...
Back to trains passing in the night
Bells ringing in the morning...
I had a double identity: A lay student sitting the H. Dip.
A cleric again for the convenience of B & B

This Is Mister M.

On my first day teaching at St. Clare's I was invited by the school Principal Sr. Bonaventure to accompany her to meet the sixth year girls at the grotto for morning prayer. I was mortified.

Girls, this is Mister M.

He has a B.A. and a H. Dip. in Education from Maynooth College.

He'll be teaching: Latin, History, English & Choir.

I am told he has a lovely singing voice.

Mister M., When you are ready ... lead us all in the hymn:

Hail Queen of Heaven.

I was truly mortified. The girls started to whisper. Whispering into each others ears. Then to laugh discreetly at first and then hysterically. All the lovely girls laughing and singing along with me:

Hail Queen Of Heaven

Milky white faced girls, all lips:

Kissing the ocean star,

Kissing the wanderer,

Kissing life's surge,

Kissing the gentle chaste and spotless Maid.

THE END

Acknowledgements

Acknowledgement is due to the editors of the following, in which a number of these poems first appeared: *The Irish Times, New Hibernia Review (*Vol. 22, No.3, University of St. Thomas, St. Paul MN), *The Stony Thursday Book* 2020, *Days of Clear Light: A Festschrift in Honour of Jessie Lendennie & in Celebration of Salmon Poetry at 40* (Salmon Poetry, 2021), *Someone Beginning with S!* An Anthology for Seamus Cashman on his 80th birthday, *The North* (issue 63, 2020), *Ogham Stone* (2020), *Teachers Who Write*, an Anthology edited by Edward Denniston (Culture Matters).

A number of poems were broadcast on RTE Lyric FM, Evelyn Grant's *Weekend Drive,* RTE.

"Cootehill" was commissioned by Cavan Arts and Poetry Ireland as part of the Nationwide's programme of appointments of Poet Laureates in 2021.

"The Theatre of Covid-19" was also commissioned by Cavan Arts.

Section no. 4 of "Let The Images Unfold" was part of a collaboration of artists: Sculptor Tom Meskell, Musicians Daragh Slake and Pat McManus and Poet Noel Monahan. This project happened during the Covid Lockdown and was organised by Cavan Arts.

Several of the poems were read on The Joe Finnegan Show, Shannonside/ Northernsound and on The Arts Programme presented by Charlie McGettigan.

A number of poems appeared on Live Encounters, http://liveencounters.net, edited by Mark Ulyseas.

Thanks to Jessie Lendennie of Salmon Poetry; Catriona O'Reilly, Cavan Arts Officer; Fergus Kennedy, Longford Arts Officer; Emma Clancy, Cavan County Librarian; Mary Carleton Reynolds, Longford County Librarian; Kevin Lavelle, for his valued advice regarding poems in Irish; Heather Brett; Enda Wyley; Dublin Windows Publications; and, Cavan County Council.

Special thanks to Pádraig Lynch for his painting which appears on the cover of this collection and to Enda Wyley for launching the book.

Thanks to Jessie Lendennie and Siobhán Hutson of Salmon Poetry.

NOEL MONAHAN is a native of Granard, Co. Longford, now living in Cavan. He has published seven collections of poetry with Salmon Poetry, with an eight collection, *Celui Qui Porte Un Veau*, a selection of French translations of his work, published in France by Alidades in 2014. A selection of Italian translations of his poetry, *Tra Una Vita E L'Altra*, was published in Milan by Guanda in 2015. His poetry was prescribed text for the Leaving Certificate English, 2011 to 2012. His play *Broken Cups* won the RTE P.J. O'Connor award in 2001 and in 2019 his long poem, *Chalk Dust*, was adapted for stage and directed by Padraic McIntyre for Ramor Theatre. During Covid-19 lockdown in 2021, Noel reinvented his poetry readings by producing a selection of short films entitled *Isolation & Creativity*, *Still Life*, *Tolle Lege* and *A Poetry Day Ireland Reading* for Cavan Library. Recently, Noel edited *Chasing Shadows*, a miscellany of poetry for Creative Ireland. *Journey Upstream* is his ninth poetry collection.

salmonpoetry
Cliffs of Moher, County Clare, Ireland

"Publishing the finest Irish and international literature."
Michael D. Higgins, President of Ireland